HOW ARE SUPERCHIPS MADE?

Technology Book for Kids 4th Grade Children's How Things Work Books

Speedy Publishing LLC

40 E. Main St. #1156

Newark, DE 19711

www.speedypublishing.com

Copyright 2018

In this book, we're going to talk about how supercars are made. So, let's get right to it!

WHAT IS A SUPERCAR?

Even car experts don't all agree on the characteristics of a supercar. However, most supercars can be described as:

- Very expensive
- Very powerful
- High performance
- Beautifully designed
- High-tech
- High-speed
- Exclusive and rare

In other words, they are the ultimate road vehicles. They are the top cars that a particular brand of car manufacturer can engineer and design.

BUGATTI VEYRON

WHICH COMPANIES MANUFACTURE SUPERCARS?

There are many companies associated with supercars. Lamborghini, W Motors, Ferrari, Bugatti, Pagani, McLaren, Aston Martin, and Mercedes are all brand names of some of the most famous supercars worldwide.

HOW IS A SUPERCAR MANUFACTURED?

When the very first cars were produced in the 1800s, they were made by hand and were very expensive. That method for creating cars completely changed when Henry Ford, the American carmaker, introduced the assembly line as a way of building cars. The goals of an assembly line were to build cars faster and to make them inexpensively enough that everyday citizens could afford to buy them.

BENZ PATENT MOTOR CAR
THE FIRST CAR IN HISTORY

FORD QUADRICYCLE

Beginning in 1913, Ford was building cars using an assembly line process. Most cars are still made this way today and sometimes pieces are assembled by robots instead of people.

However, just as supercars break the rules for how cars look and perform, they also break the rules for how they are constructed.

BENZ PATENT MOTOR CAR

NO ASSEMBLY LINES FOR SUPERCARS

Supercars are not manufactured on high-speed assembly lines. Although there are areas of specialization, a supercar is built solely by hand and it takes a long time to build. On average, it takes about half a year or longer for a supercar to be built. At one time, a production facility might handle 10 or 12 cars.

CAR ASSEMBLY LINE

BUGATTI CHIRON

The car manufacturer can afford to build so few cars at a time because these are cars for wealthy people. They often have price tags in the millions. Every brand of supercar is built differently so we'll look at details on how the Bugatti Chiron is built. It will give you an idea of the specific process needed to build a supercar that meets the ultimate standards of performance and quality.

The Bugatti is made in France and its parent company is Volkswagen. The company has a high-tech production facility for the Bugatti Chiron in the city of Molsheim, which is in the northeastern section of France. They call this facility the "atelier," which means "studio."

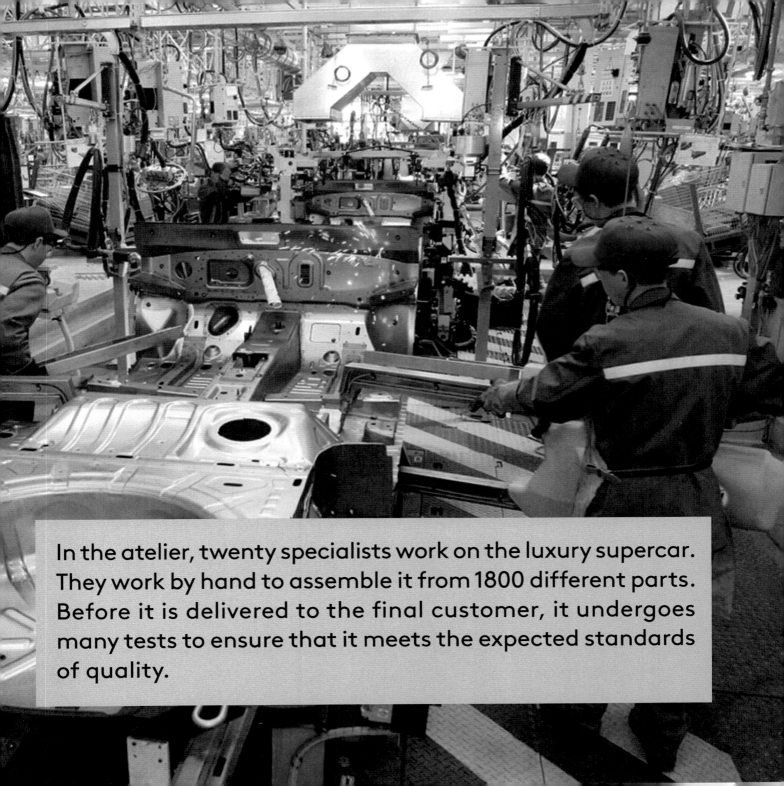

In the atelier, twenty specialists work on the luxury supercar. They work by hand to assemble it from 1800 different parts. Before it is delivered to the final customer, it undergoes many tests to ensure that it meets the expected standards of quality.

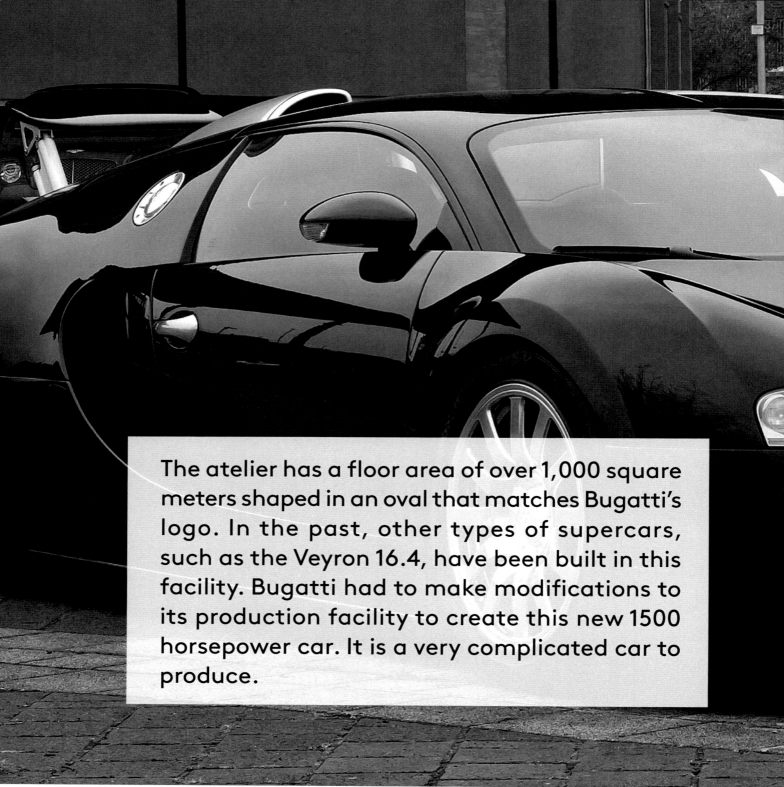

The atelier has a floor area of over 1,000 square meters shaped in an oval that matches Bugatti's logo. In the past, other types of supercars, such as the Veyron 16.4, have been built in this facility. Bugatti had to make modifications to its production facility to create this new 1500 horsepower car. It is a very complicated car to produce.

BUGATTI VEYRON

A CUSTOMER ORDERS THE CUSTOMIZED SUPERCAR

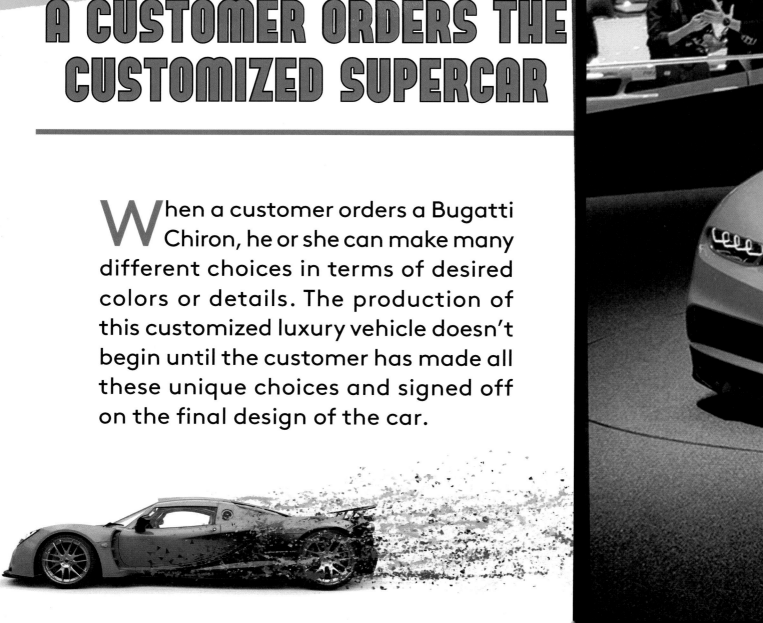

When a customer orders a Bugatti Chiron, he or she can make many different choices in terms of desired colors or details. The production of this customized luxury vehicle doesn't begin until the customer has made all these unique choices and signed off on the final design of the car.

BUGATTI CHIRON

Sun
Mon
Tue
Wed
Thu
Fri
Sat
29
1
3
4
5
5
6
7
9
11
12
13
14
18
19
20
21
24
25
26
27
28
31
1
2
3

Of course, if the customer has made many unusual requests, the timeline for the final delivery of the car will need to be extended. It will take from 6 to 9 months for the entire process from customer signoff to the finished Bugatti Chiron.

A PRODUCTION TIMESLOT IS DETERMINED

Next, the parts for the supercar are ordered from the suppliers. For Bugatti, these suppliers are located in many places throughout Europe. The parts are custom as well and the suppliers work diligently to get them to the atelier so that production can begin.

THE ASSEMBLY OF THE BODYSHELL

P rior to production beginning, about one month before, the bodyshell of the supercar is put together with the monocoque, which is a solid piece including the chassis, and the substructure of the chassis. Once everything is tested to ensure that the pieces fit together perfectly, the next step is the paint.

LAYERS AND LAYERS OF PAINT AND POLISH

Depending on what type of finish the customer has ordered, there may be up to eight individual layers or more of paint in a metallic finish or pearlescent finish for the top coat. The process is very time-consuming and takes about three weeks. The layers are painted by hand and each coat of paint must be sanded as well as polished before the subsequent coat of paint can be added.

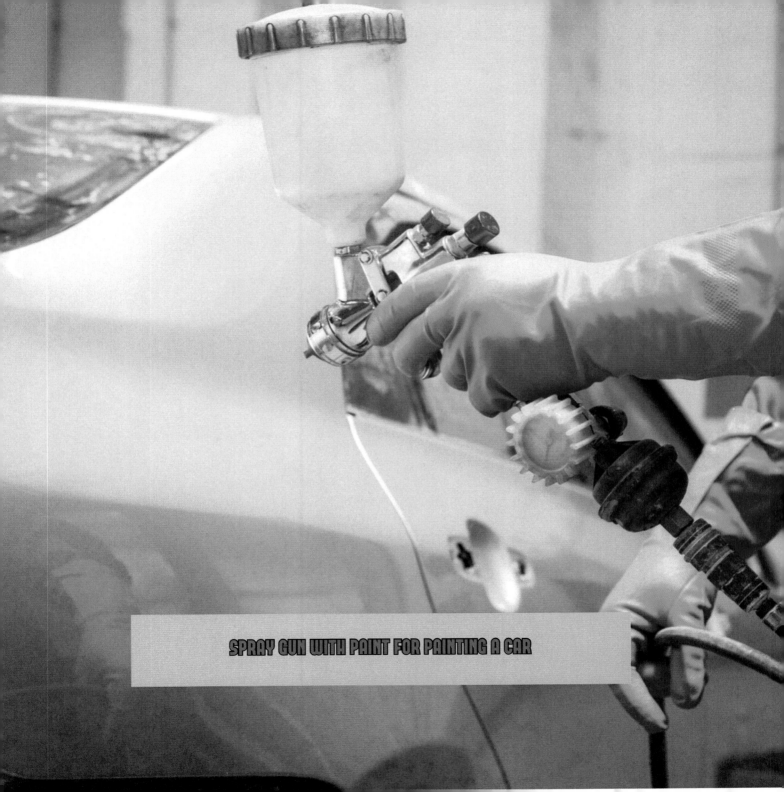

SPRAY GUN WITH PAINT FOR PAINTING A CAR

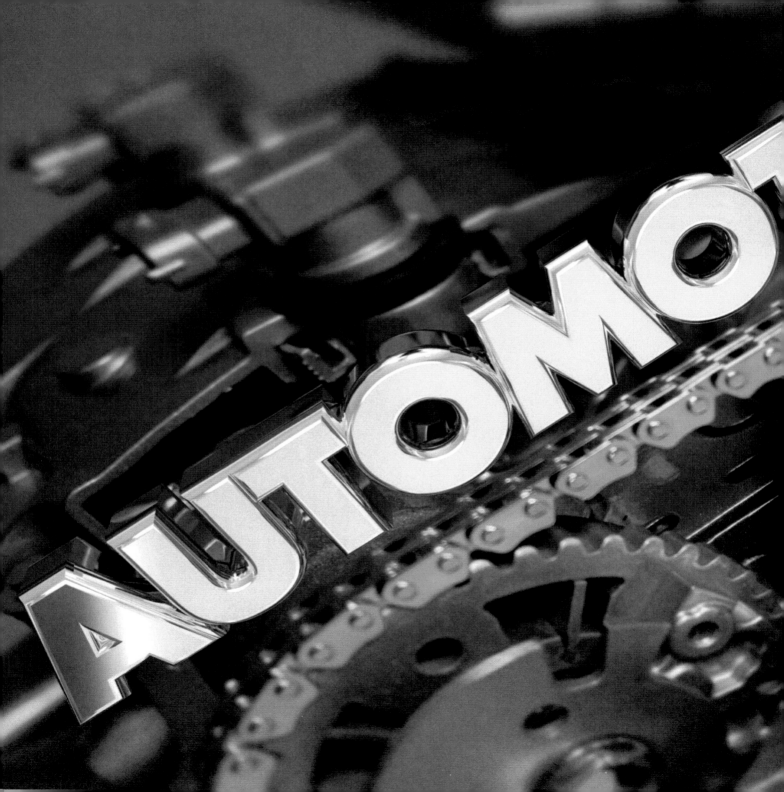

THE POWERTRAIN

There aren't any robotic arms or conveyor belts at the Molsheim production facility. The people work at specialized stations. There are a dozen different stations. The first is where the powertrain, the 1500 horsepower engine, is readied for the process of assembly.

It comes already assembled from the Volkswagen plant in the city of Salzgitter where it is built in a special hall that is used only for Bugatti. It is tested for quality for a full eight hours before it is shipped to Molsheim.

A similar process is used for the dual-clutch transmission, which has 7 speeds. The transmission has been constructed both larger and stronger than types used for previous supercars, to withstand the

enormous power output of the car. The Bugatti Chiron has an amazing torque capability of 1600 Nm, which means that it has a twisting force of 1600 Newton meters.

ATTACHING THE REAR END OF THE VEHICLE TO THE ENGINE

In the atelier, there are two platforms designated for the next stage of the assembly. The vehicle's rear end is constructed around the engine. At that same time, the monocoque is joined with the front end of the vehicle. Another critical step is the connection of pipes at the rear of the engine to radiators located in the front.

Because of the Chiron's massive amount of power, it requires special water pumps to keep it cooled down. There are three such pumps. One is allocated for the cycles of

high-temperature and two are for the cycles of low-temperature. Three of Bugatti's employees spend a full week on this part of the process.

The only electronic tool that is used is a special tool that measures the tightness of the bolts. It keeps data stored on a computer that measures the correct torque value for each of the 1800 bolts. The most critical part of the assembly of the chassis is the bonding of the monocoque and the vehicle's rear end, which is joined with fourteen ultra-strong, lightweight bolts made of titanium. The bolts only weigh 34 grams each, but they are amazingly strong. Supercars must have lightweight construction in order to attain the highest speeds possible.

THE SEVENTH STEP
THE DYNAMOMETER

A dynamometer is an instrument designed to measure the power of an engine. This was the section of the production facility that needed the most re-tooling to test the Chiron. The previous dynamometer wasn't powerful enough to test this new supercar.

CAR DYNAMOMETER

THE ROLLERS OF A MODERN DYNAMOMETER ROLLING ROAD.

The new dynamometer is the most powerful in the world. It can produce electrical current up to 1200 amps when it's operating. In fact, it produces so much power that the extra electricity is sent to the local power grid in the city of Molsheim. The supercar must pass a number of very strict tests on the dynamometer. Once it passes these tests, it moves on to the next step.

TRADITIONAL ALSATIAN HOUSES IN MOLSHEIM - BAS-RHIN, FRANCE

THE EIGHTH STEP
THE EXTERIOR SKIN

At this stage, all the exterior pieces are placed in their correct positions on the vehicle. These pieces are lightweight, large, and somewhat fragile. The work is very demanding. Every part must be inspected for defects or damage before it is installed.

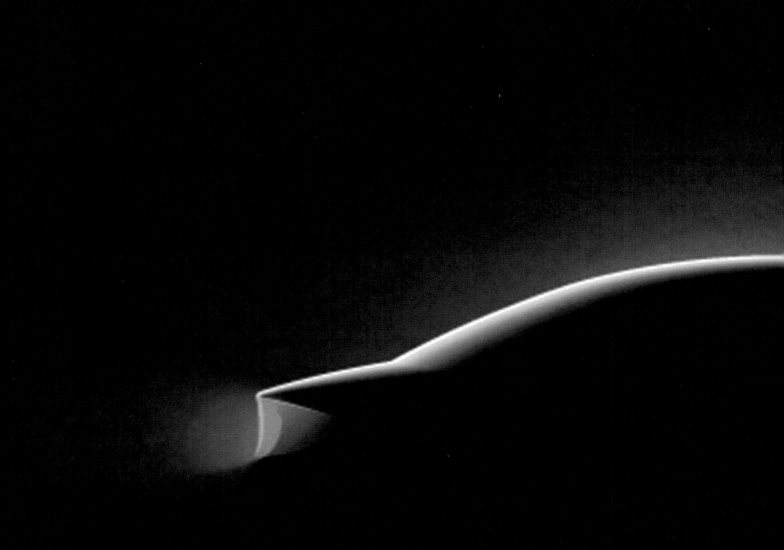

The process takes about four days and once everything is installed, all the joints are inspected. This process takes place about 200 meters away from the atelier in a brand-new,

THE NINTH STEP
THE MONSOON WATER TEST

Next, the vehicle is subjected to monsoon-level rain for more than 30 minutes to ensure that there isn't the slightest leak on the inside. Once it passes that test, the luxurious interiors are put into position. This process takes up to four days.

A SUPERCAR UNDERGOES A MONSOON WATER TEST TO PREVENT THE SCENE IN THE PHOTO FROM HAPPENING

THE TENTH STEP
THE SPEED TEST

After a few other adjustments are made, the vehicle leaves the production facility where it is taken for a test drive of 300 kilometers through the Vosges Mountains on the way to the airport of Colmar. During the drive, it goes through various tests and at times is driven at speeds of over 250 kilometers per hour.

If the driver gives his or her approval, then the car undergoes a final test drive of 50 kilometers.

The Bugatti can go from a standing start to 400 kilometers per hour back to a stationary position in 42 seconds.

BUGATTI VEYRON

THE ELEVENTH STEP
FINAL FINISH

The Bugatti team of men and women do a final inspection of the paint and polish of the supercar and any final blemishes are fixed before this amazing supercar leaves the facility.

SUMMARY

Supercars are evolving in speed and performance all the time. These ultimate driving machines are built to very high levels of quality and they are crafted by hand instead of using the assembly line process typical for building ordinary cars. These types of cars cost millions of dollars to buy. Wealthy customers can request many custom features on their supercars before they are built, but they must be patient once they order their cars. These luxury cars take 6 to 9 months to build and test before customers can drive them on the open road.

Awesome! Now that you've read about supercars, you may want to read about race cars in the Baby Professor book How Do Race Cars Work? Car Book for Kids | Children's Transportation Books.

Visit

BABY PROFESSOR
EDUCATION KIDS

www.BabyProfessorBooks.com

to download Free Baby Professor eBooks
and view our catalog of new and exciting
Children's Books

Made in the USA
Las Vegas, NV
23 October 2021